My Little Golden Book About
CATS

By Joanne Ryder
Illustrated by Dora Leder

A Golden Book · New York
Western Publishing Company, Inc., Racine, Wisconsin 53404

The illustrations in this book depict a charming story not directly related to the text, which is factual.

We think that parents and children will enjoy creating their own stories to follow the illustrations.

Read Grandma's letter to begin the story.

Dear Sue and Dave,
Molly has had four
kittens. You can see
them on your next
visit. Love,
Grandma

When a kitten is born, it cannot see or hear. But it can smell its mother, and it may feel her warm, soft body gently move as she purrs and purrs. By smell and touch, the tiny kitten stays close to her.

At first the kitten just drinks its mother's milk
and sleeps. Gradually its eyes begin to open.
Then it begins to hear sounds.

It can hear its mother's rumbling purr now.
It can see and hear you, too.

Kittens are small and fragile. But as they begin to grow and get stronger, you can touch them and hold them gently.

You may handle a growing kitten carefully for a few minutes every day. The kitten will learn and grow faster. It will learn to like being touched, and it will grow up to be a better pet.

When a young cat is several weeks old, it is ready to explore its world. Creeping toward a paper ball, a young cat moves like a hunter. Like a tiny tiger, it creeps closer and then leaps. It catches the ball just as a tiger would catch its meal.

All cats leap and run and jump and climb. They are fast and powerful and graceful.

As a kitten grows it needs to eat more. It laps up milk with its tiny tongue. It begins to eat meat.

Cats are meat eaters. Their front teeth are long and sharp. They are the teeth of a hunter. Their side teeth cut like scissors. Cats do not chew their food like you do. They slice it into little pieces to swallow.

Cats learn from their mothers to keep their fur clean. A cat's tongue is rough. By licking its fur, a cat combs and cleans it.

This Manx cat has no tail. But it has long back legs. It runs with a rabbitlike hop.

This Siamese cat has short hair and a thin body. Its face and ears are long. Its fur is creamy brown, yet darker brown on its paws, face, and tail.

A striped cat is called a tabby.

A Persian cat has long fluffy hair. It has a big round head and a short snub nose.

Cats are born with a soft coat of fur. A cat's fur can be long or short, many colors or one color.

In the winter a thick coat of fur keeps a cat warm. To thin out its coat a cat sheds some of its fur. In the summer a cat's coat is lighter and cooler.

Most cats have long furry tails. When a cat leaps, it uses its long tail to keep its balance.

Though all cats are the same in some ways, there are many different *kinds* of cats.

A cat has whiskers—long hairs on its face. These whiskers touch nearby things. They may help a cat feel its way when it is too dark to see.

A cat walks softly on its padded toes. When it walks, a cat hides its claws inside its paws. But when it stretches, it spreads its sharp claws. Cats use their claws when hunting, climbing, and fighting.

When a cat scratches a tree or post, it is sharpening its claws. The cat is also leaving scent marks on the spot. Cats mark their part of the world with their scent.

Sometimes a cat may rub its face and body against you. The cat is marking you. You cannot smell the cat's mark, but another cat can smell it.

Stare into a cat's eyes and see who blinks first!
A cat does not need to blink to protect its eyes,
like you do. If a light is turned on, the cat's pupils
quickly close to small slits. Just the right
amount of light enters the cat's eyes.

In the dark the cat's pupils open very wide and let in more light. This helps it see better.

A cat can hear sounds you cannot hear. It can hear the very high calls of mice or insects. When a cat listens, it turns its large pointed ears toward the sound it hears.

Some cats live on their own. They hunt for food in city streets and country meadows. Other cats work keeping farms and shops free of mice and rats. But many cats live with people as pets. A cat can be a playful and loving pet.

A pet cat needs fresh food and water every day. It needs a litter box, a scratching post, and a warm, safe place to sleep. A pet cat that is well cared for may live for many years.

When you meet a cat, wait and let it come to you. It may sniff your fingers. It may rub against you. It may choose you and mark you gently as part of its world.

Gently touch your new friend. Feel its soft fur. Feel its rough tongue tickle your skin. And listen. Listen for the sound that tells you this cat is pleased with your touch. Listen to it purr.

When a cat purrs like this, it is feeling friendly.